# Close Enough To Break

The weight of things unsaid

Kenneth Neider

India | USA | UK

Copyright © Kenneth Neider
All Rights Reserved.

This book has been self-published with all reasonable efforts taken to make the material error-free by the author. No part of this book shall be used, reproduced in any manner whatsoever without written permission from the author, except in the case of brief quotations embodied in critical articles and reviews.

The Author of this book is solely responsible and liable for its content including but not limited to the views, representations, descriptions, statements, information, opinions, and references ["Content"]. The Content of this book shall not constitute or be construed or deemed to reflect the opinion or expression of the Publisher or Editor. Neither the Publisher nor Editor endorse or approve the Content of this book or guarantee the reliability, accuracy, or completeness of the Content published herein and do not make any representations or warranties of any kind, express or implied, including but not limited to the implied warranties of merchantability, fitness for a particular purpose.

The Publisher and Editor shall not be liable whatsoever...

Made with ❤ on the BookLeaf Publishing Platform
www.bookleafpub.in
www.bookleafpub.com

# Dedication

For the one who never had to try. Your presence was everything.

# Preface

Foreword

I didn't set out to write a book.

I wrote because I had nowhere else to put the things I was feeling; no room left inside me for the weight of what went unsaid. These pages aren't fiction. They're fragments. Memories. Moments I lived and carried long after they passed.

This is a story told in pieces; of friendship that felt like gravity, of love that was never named out loud, of the silence that followed when everything finally broke open. It's about what happens when you see someone so clearly, and love them not in spite of their flaws, but because of them. And then feel as if you're losing them. Some of these poems were written in the thick of it. Some came after. All of them are true.

This isn't a story with a clean ending. It's not about getting the girl or walking away stronger. It's about staying. About showing up. About loving someone even when they don't know how to choose you back and learning how to choose yourself in the aftermath.

If you've ever held your heart out quietly
and been met with silence,
this is for you.
If you've ever loved someone in a way

you couldn't quite name,
this is for you.
And if you're still standing
with a chest full of ache
and no one left to tell;
this is for you most of all.
—Ken

# Acknowledgements

This book is stitched together from the quiet places;
the nights I didn't think I'd survive,
the silences that shaped me,
and the love that cracked me open in ways I'll never
forget.

It's a testament to what happens
when two people get close enough to change each other
in ways neither could expect.

These pages hold the ache I carried in the dark,
the words I swallowed to keep the peace,
the prayers I whispered into empty rooms,
and the fragments of a man learning
that heartbreak isn't the end of love;
just the place where it changes form.

To the woman who taught me what it means
to love without asking for anything back:
thank you for the light,
for the laughter,
for the kind of presence that becomes a compass
long after the moment has passed.

And to the version of myself
who held on,
let go,
broke,
and rebuilt;
this is your story too.

May these poems honor what was real,
grieve what was lost,
and bless what remains.

# Part 1: The Spark In The Quiet. The Shattering

I don't talk much about that year.
The year everything shattered
like a glass on a rock;
quiet first,
then all at once.
I was a man made of routines,
of bedtime stories,
of morning coffee kissed by tired affection.
I wore love like a jacket I'd broken in,
soft in the elbows,
frayed in the corners,
familiar even when it didn't quite fit anymore.
But comfort can be a liar.
And silence can be sharp
when it finally speaks.
I walked in on the truth.
Not whispered.
Not confessed.
Just... there.

A blade mid-swing.
A moment I'll never be able to unsee.
After that,
I lived in the quiet aftermath.
A man trying to father children
while bleeding out invisibly.
I made peanut butter sandwiches with shaking hands.
I held bedtime together
with the kind of calm
you only learn in warzones.
Grief didn't knock.
It moved in.
Sat on my chest at night.
Stole the color from things.
Made me question
if I was still real.
If anything ever had been.
I wasn't looking for hope.
I didn't believe in it then.
I just wanted to make it to the next morning
without falling apart in front of my kids.
That was the version of me then.
Not a man.
Not a hero.
Just a wreck
still standing.

# Part I: The Spark in the Quiet. Longing In Disguise

The excuse was the children.
Playdates.
School pickups.
Little hands reaching for each other
like it was the most natural thing in the world.
So we let them.
And in letting them,
we let ourselves inch closer;
under the guise of convenience,
of co-parenting kindness,
of "It's good for the kids."
But the truth is;
it became good for us, too.
I started looking forward to the sound of her car pulling in.
To the soft knock on the door.
To the way her eyes smiled before her mouth ever did.
We still pretended it was nothing.
Two adults in orbit

around two children
who had no idea
they were holding the blueprint
for a bridge we'd forgotten how to build.
We traded laughter like it was spare change.
We lingered longer in thresholds
than the situation required.
I started folding extra snacks into my son's lunch
because I knew he might share.
And I hoped maybe that meant
we still had something left to offer, too.
It wasn't flirting.
It wasn't love.
It was longing dressed in manners.
A light in the dark,
small but steady,
inviting us to sit by the fire
without asking how long we'd been cold.

# Part I: The Spark in the Quiet. The Quiet That Hums

There's a kind of quiet
nobody talks about.
Not the peaceful kind;
not stillness.
This one hums.
Like an old lightbulb
flickering in an empty room.
It lives in the spaces
between custody exchanges,
between dinners made for kids
you barely had the strength to show up for.
I wasn't living.
I was performing.
Smiling on instinct.
Nodding through meetings,
through pickups,
through breakdowns in grocery store aisles
no one ever saw.
I didn't have anyone left

who really knew how I used to laugh.
How I used to believe in things.
Grief made the world feel muffled.
Like I was shouting underwater.
Like everything I reached for
slipped through my hands.
I wasn't angry anymore.
Not really.
Anger burned hot.
I had gone cold.
What hurt the most
was not the betrayal;
not even the loneliness.
It was the vanishing.
The way I disappeared
from the center of my own life
and no one noticed.

I didn't want to be saved.
I didn't believe in that type of thing anymore.

I just wanted
Someone to sit beside me
Without asking me to explain.

# Part I: The Spark in the Quiet. Recognition

She never asked questions I wasn't ready to answer.
Never forced smiles
or filled silence with noise
just to make it easier to breathe.
She just...
sat with me.
In the mess.
In the mundane.
Like it wasn't strange to share sadness
without naming it.
We became something unspoken.
Comfort in passing.
A glance in the hallway
that said more than entire conversations.
She had this way
of folding herself into the quiet
without vanishing.
Of showing up
without needing anything back.

I didn't know what to call it then.
Friendship? Maybe.
But it felt older than that.
Like we'd met before;
some other life,
some unfinished sentence
we were still writing in this one.
She never once said
"I see how broken you are."
But I swear she did.
Not with pity.
Not with fear.
Just a kind of
tender recognition;
the way survivors recognize each other
without having to swap war stories.
And slowly,
without touching a single brick,
she became part of the foundation
I was rebuilding.
Not love.
Not yet.
But something steady.
Something sacred.

# Part I: The Spark in the Quiet. Before I Knew Her Name

It started on a balcony;
not the romantic kind,
just cold concrete, fake wood and metal,
a place where tired people pause
between errands and unraveling.
I was holding my kid,
thinking about groceries, bills,
how many cracks a man could carry
before something finally gave,
when a little voice floated up from the sidewalk:
"That's my friend!"
I looked down.
And saw her.
Not the child;
the woman beside her.
We locked eyes.
Two strangers,

two parents
faking calm for the sake of small hands.
And something...
shifted.
Not loudly.
Not like a movie.
Just;
true.
She smiled,
not the kind meant to charm,
but the kind that doesn't ask anything of you.
The kind that meets you in your unraveling
and still sees something whole.
Her laugh
when it came
was the sound of someone remembering
what it felt like to be light.
It didn't heal me.
But it cracked something open
that had been rusted shut.
There was no exchange of names,
no introductions.
Just the quiet gravity
of someone who noticed
without needing to be noticed back.
I didn't know it then,
but that moment;

that smile beside a child
calling to another;
was the start of something
I would carry for years.
Not a love story.
Not yet.
Just a flicker.
A breath.
A beginning.

# Part I: The Spark in the Quiet. If This Was Just Friendship

We were just friends, right?
Just two people who couldn't stop
finding excuses to be there.
Late nights on porches,
talking about everything and nothing,
laughing like the world wasn't burning behind us.
We made questionable decisions
and called them therapy.
Took turns losing our minds,
held space like bodyguards
for each other's worst days.
You watched me face hell with my teeth bared.
I watched you drink ghosts and swallow rage.
We never flinched.
We never judged.
We just showed up.
There were nights out in the quiet

no clocks, no city lights,
just us and the dark
and the crackle of some half-dead fire
burning down to truth.
You beside me,
shoulders barely brushing,
but it felt like the world was holding still
just long enough for us to breathe again.
You were the calm in my chaos.
The trouble I trusted.
The echo that answered back.
And yeah
we were just friends.
But if that's true,
then friendship
might be the holiest thing
I've ever known.

# Part I: The Spark in the Quiet. The Shift

There wasn't a single moment.
No grand realization.
Just this slow, steady ache
that started showing up
every time you smiled at me like that.
One day I noticed
I was listening harder when you spoke.
Laughing longer.
Tucking away your words
like they were tools I'd need later.
I stopped comparing you to anyone else.
Because no one else ever came close.
The shift was quiet
a glance held too long,
the way your name sounded softer in my mouth.
A touch on my shoulder
that felt like it reached my chest
and stayed there.
I'd sit across from you

trying to play it cool
while my insides
burned to memorize every angle of your face.
I knew your tells.
Your tired eyes.
Your brave laugh.
And the way you held the whole damn world
without asking for help,
but screamed for it with your eyes.
It hit me one night
some late hour,
just the two of us and the dark.
I looked over and thought,
"God, she's beautiful."
Not just the way she looks.
But the way she is.
And I knew, right then,
this wasn't friendship anymore.
Not for me.
I didn't say it.
Didn't show it.
But it lived in me after that.
Set up camp.
Started rewiring every part of how I saw you.
And from that moment on,
everything got louder
inside me

every time you called me
Friend

# Part I: The Spark in the Quiet. Almost Something

It was never said aloud.
Not then.
Not even close.
But I kept showing up
for reasons I didn't know how to name.
And I started noticing things
that weren't mine to hold onto.
The quiet between us
began to stretch
not in distance,
but in weight.
I never said what I was feeling.
Didn't ask if she felt it too.
I just... carried it.
Let it live in the way I lingered,
in the way I listened,
in the way I replayed our moments
long after they passed.
It wasn't anything,

but it wasn't nothing either.
Her presence made the world feel softer.
Not brighter.
Just less sharp.
And that was enough to keep me coming back.
I wasn't in love;
not officially.
There was nothing to prove,
nothing to confess.
But sometimes my heart ached
in her direction,
and I didn't have the courage
or the right
to ask why.
So I stayed
inside the quiet.
Inside the questions.
Inside the almost
that only I could feel.

# Part I: The Spark in the Quiet. What We Never Said

There were things I never said.
Things I buried beneath casual smiles
and practical conversations.
Things I folded into small moments
like notes left in coat pockets
I hoped someone might find
but never dared to place directly in their hand.
There were times I thought she might feel it too.
But I never asked.
Never reached for clarity.
Because some truths,
once spoken,
can't be taken back.
So I sat with mine.
Quietly.
Carefully.
Letting them bloom behind my ribs
where no one else could see.
There were pauses in our conversations

that felt like cliff edges.
Like maybe,
just maybe,
we were both standing there
waiting for the other to jump.
But I couldn't be sure.
And I couldn't afford the fall.
So I stayed silent.
And so did she.
We built something real.
Whatever it was.
Whatever name it could have had
in a different world.
But love unspoken
is still love.
And silence doesn't make it less true.
I never told her
what she meant to me.
Not really.
Not until long after
the space between us had grown too wide to reach
across.
And by then,
what we never said
had already become
what we never were.

# Part I: The Spark in the Quiet. Waiting Without Asking

I got used to waiting
without asking.
To hoping
without making demands of the world
or of her.
It wasn't patience.
Not really.
It was something quieter.
More fragile.
A kind of sacred endurance
I didn't have a name for.
I told myself I was just being careful.
Respectful.
But truthfully,
I was afraid.
Afraid of knowing
what she didn't feel.

Afraid of naming something
she might never have seen at all.
So I stayed where I was;
on the edges.
Close enough to feel her warmth,
never close enough to be burned.
I learned to treasure the smallest things.
A shared glance.
A text that made me laugh out loud.
The way her voice softened
when we were the last ones still talking.
And maybe that should have been enough.
Sometimes it was.
Other times it cracked me open
in places no one could see.
I never asked for more.
Never reached.
Never confessed.
But I loved her
in the way a shoreline loves the sea;
always touched,
never held.

# Part II: Love in Disguise.
# The Softest Ruin

I didn't tell her everything.
Not even close.
Just enough to feel like I'd finally opened the door
without blowing the house down.
I kept the sharpest parts to myself;
the years of quiet ache,
the way her absence felt like frostbite,
the dreams I'd dared to imagine with her in them.
I gave her a version
that was safe,
honest,
but softened.
Wrapped in disclaimers
and careful language
like I was handing her something fragile
and didn't want her to know it was actually my heart.
I told her I cared.
That something had changed.
That I didn't know what to do with the weight

of wanting more than just late-night conversations
and quiet companionship.
And she...
she was kind.
But distant.
Said she wasn't sure.
That she wasn't where I was.
That she didn't want to lose what we already had.
I heard fear in her voice.
Or maybe uncertainty.
Or maybe that's just what I needed to believe
to survive the sound of her pulling back.
She didn't run.
She didn't reach.
She just stood still.
And in that stillness,
I started to sink.
Not because she rejected me;
but because I finally said it out loud
and nothing around me changed.
The sky didn't fall.
The world didn't break open.
But something in me did.
Quietly.
Permanently.
It wasn't the end.
Not yet.

Just the beginning
of letting go.

# Part II: Love in Disguise. The Last Way I Knew How to Love You

It wasn't anger.
It wasn't a fight.
Just a quiet reckoning
that we weren't standing on the same side of this anymore.
I kept trying to meet her where she was.
But the road started curving
in directions I couldn't follow
without losing myself.
So I left.
Not because I stopped caring;
God, no.
I left because I cared so fucking much
it was starting to unmake me.
She was still in my phone,
still in my blood,
still in the empty passenger seat.

But I couldn't keep breaking myself
against her unreadiness.
And maybe she couldn't meet me in that place.
Maybe she didn't even know I'd gone.
But I felt it.
Like something sacred
tearing just beneath the surface.
I walked away
not to punish her,
but to protect what little I had left.
To protect her, too;
from the weight of my quiet suffering.
I told myself it was strength.
That choosing myself was survival.
But every mile I put between us
tasted like grief.
Because no matter how many reasons I had,
no matter how necessary it was,
letting go of her
was the closest I've ever come
To dying without dying.

# Part II: Love in Disguise. Missing You Quietly

You think silence will bring peace.
That distance will cool the fire,
that if you stop showing up,
your heart will follow suit.
It doesn't.
It just gets quieter.
And somehow,
the quiet hurts worse.
I kept checking my phone.
Not expecting you to reach out,
just hoping.
Like maybe you'd feel it,
that echo where I used to be.
The nights were the worst.
No voice.
No soft laugh bleeding through the line.
Just the sound of my own thoughts
getting louder with every minute
you weren't there to interrupt them.

The world kept going.
Bills got paid.
Work got done.
I even smiled at people
like nothing inside me had collapsed.
But underneath it all,
I was still holding your place.
Like a seat at the table
I couldn't bring myself to clear.
I told myself you were probably fine.
That maybe you didn't miss me.
And that; somehow, hurt worse
than the missing itself.
I didn't want to come back.
I needed to.
But I waited.
Longer than I should have.
Because pride can sound a lot like survival
when your soul's been split open.
And even then
even in that hollow, aching space
I never stopped hoping
you'd miss me too.

# Part II: Love in Disguise. Everyone Who Wasn't Her

There was healing, I think.
Or something that looked like it.
Other women.
Brief, bright flings.
Romance that burned fast
and left no smoke behind.
They laughed at my jokes.
Held my hand.
Said all the right things.
And for a while, I let them.
Let them close enough to forget
for an hour,
a night,
sometimes even a week.
But they weren't her.
They never could be.
I tried not to compare
but she was always there
in the space between touches.

In the quiet after the kiss.
In the mornings that didn't feel like anything.
I smiled.
I moved forward.
I even thought I was better for a time.
Then I heard she'd moved on.
Someone new.
Someone else.
And it hit like it shouldn't.
Like I'd swallowed a blade
I thought I'd already spat out.
I didn't rage.
Didn't reach out.
Didn't say a word.
But something sank in me that day
not jealousy,
not anger
just the deep, cold ache
of knowing she was learning
how to laugh with someone else.
And all I could do
was keep pretending
that I'd stopped remembering
how her smile felt
in the moments
when it belonged
to me.

# Part II: Love in Disguise. I Carried Her Anyway

I never met him.
Didn't need to.
All I saw was the way
she stood a little differently
with someone else at her side.
I watched from the outside
no right to feel it,
but feeling it anyway.
Not rage.
Not envy.
Just that hollow pressure in my chest
where her name still lived.
He got the parts of her
I used to read between the lines.
Her late-night thoughts,
her coffee orders,
that quiet tilt of her head and press of her lips when
she's thinking too much
but doesn't want to say it out loud.

He didn't earn those.
But they were his now.
And I smiled.
I fucking smiled
because that's what you do
when you've lost something
you never really had.
I wondered if he knew
how much she laughs when she's nervous,
or that she stares out of car windows like she's
somewhere else,
far away.
I wondered if he held her right.
Or if she pulled away
when the lights went out.
Part of me hoped he was good to her.
The other part
hoped he wasn't.
Because if he hurt her,
at least I'd understand the ending.
I dated too.
Slept next to strangers
with warm skin and colder hearts.
Told myself I was moving on
even as I kept hearing her name
in places it didn't belong.
And through it all,

she was out there
living, laughing, loving
like I'd never been a chapter,
just a footnote in her story.
I never reached out.
But I never really let go.
Because while he stood beside her...
I still carried her.

# Part II: Love in Disguise. When Love Goes Inward

I stopped writing you
in half-finished thoughts
and imagined conversations
no one else would ever hear.
Stopped rehearsing the moment
you might look at me
and finally understand.
But I never stopped
carrying it.
The love.
The want.
The softness that built itself around you
like muscle around bone.
It just lives quieter now.
In the pauses between my sentences.
In the dreams I don't talk about.
In the way I still reach
for someone who isn't there.
It doesn't ask for anything anymore.

Not your voice.
Not your return.
Not even your memory.
It just stays.
Like an echo
without a room to bounce in.
I don't know if you ever knew.
If you ever felt it.
But I did.
Fully.
Brutally.
Without condition.
And maybe that's the thing
about love like this;
When it has nowhere left to go,
it goes inward.
It becomes part of who you are.
Not something you give;
just something you carry.

# Part III: The Return. When The World Broke Her Open

I used to dream of her reaching out.
Of my phone lighting up
with her name and something simple like
"Hey... you free?"
But I stopped waiting.
Stopped hoping.
Learned how to quiet that part of me
that still answered every silence with her name.
And then one day;
she did.
No warning.
No buildup.
Just a message that hit harder
than any goodbye ever had.
Things had fallen apart.
Not with me.
With him.
And in the wreckage,
when the dust finally cleared,

she looked around
and reached for me.
Like her heart still remembered
where safety lived.
And I'd be lying if I said
I didn't hesitate.
Because love doesn't just sit in the corner
waiting patiently to be chosen.
It hardens.
It hides.
It learns to protect itself.
But all that melted the second I heard her voice again.
That voice that never changed.
That laughter that still cracked something open
and poured light in where I thought nothing could grow.
She didn't need fixing.
She just needed presence.
And I showed up
like I always had.
Like no time had passed
and no pain had built between us.
But something had changed.
This wasn't me chasing anymore.
This was her
reaching back.
Not for rescue.
Not out of regret.

Just to say:
"You're still the one I trust
when everything else burns."

# Part III: The Return. The Floor She Fell Apart On

Her name lit up my screen
and my whole body forgot how to breathe.
It wasn't joy.
It wasn't pain.
It was both.
A storm in the chest.
A wildfire in the ribs.
Everything I'd buried
rising all at once.
She was hurting.
You could hear it in the silence
between her words.
In the way she hesitated;
like maybe I'd slam the door
she once left open.
But I didn't.
I never could.
She talked.
Told me everything that broke her.

And I listened.
Not as the man who still loved her;
but as the friend who never stopped being one.
My mind was a whirlwind;
spinning with things I didn't say:
"I missed you."
"I still think of you."
"Say the word and I'll drive through hell again."
But I didn't say any of it.
I just listened.
Because that's what she needed.
Not my desire.
Not my hope.
Just my presence.
And God, my heart was screaming.
It caught fire the second she said my name again.
But I swallowed every flame.
Let her speak.
Let her hurt.
Let her remember
what it felt like to be safe.
I could've asked why now.
I could've told her what it cost me
to hear her voice
and not reach across that line.
But I didn't.
I just held space.

Quiet.
Solid.
There.
Because when someone you love
comes back broken;
you don't hand them pieces of yourself.
You become the floor
they can fall apart on.

# Part III: The Return. Gravity Between Us

We met in the park
under the guise of the kids.
Old routines dressed as coincidence,
like we weren't both
waiting for this to happen
long before the message was sent.
It was awkward at first.
Safe smiles.
Measured steps.
Like two people
tiptoeing through the memory of something
they never quite got to live.
And then;
the hug.
Just a few seconds.
Polite.
Casual.
But not really.
Because my body remembered her

before my mind had the courage to admit it.
Her arms fit the same way they always had;
like the silence between us had been waiting
to be held again.
We walked.
I felt everything.
The bump of her shoulder against mine,
the way our hands almost brushed
and neither of us pulled away.
The slight lean when she laughed too hard.
The way I found myself
angling toward her
like gravity was something we'd invented together.
I didn't want it to end.
Any of it.
Not the walk.
Not the warmth.
Not the feeling that,
for a brief moment,
I was exactly where I was supposed to be.
We said our goodbyes
like we weren't both aching
to stay just a little longer.
And for the rest of the day,
I could still feel
the shape of her arms

>  wrapped around me
>  like a story we still hadn't told.

# Part III: The Return. Like Nothing and Everything

It didn't come rushing back.
No flood, no spark.
Just a slow drip
of old familiarity
finding its way
through new cracks.
A message here.
A photo there.
A sentence that lingered
a little longer than it used to.
Not enough to mean anything;
but enough to make me feel again.
At first, it was weeks between replies.
Light things.
Casual.
Safe.
Like we were circling something unspoken
but not ready to name it.
And I didn't read into it.

Didn't let myself.
Still, there were moments;
a laugh,
a pause,
a "glad you're here"
that felt like it carried
something just beneath the surface.
But I never asked.
Never pushed.
Because I didn't know if it was there,
or if I just wanted it to be.
I stayed steady.
Careful.
Present.
Listening like I always had,
but guarding the parts of me
that used to lean in too hard, too fast.
Some nights, I'd go to sleep
with her voice still echoing;
not in my ears,
but in the quiet part of me
that still remembered
what closeness felt like
before it hurt.
And slowly, the space between us
started to close.
Not every night;

not yet;
but more than before.
And every time we spoke,
it felt like nothing.
Like friendship.
Like normal.
But also;
something.
Something just out of reach.
Something I couldn't prove,
but couldn't ignore either.
So I stayed.
Not chasing.
Not assuming.
Just... staying.
Because sometimes,
being there
is the only way to know
if what you felt
was ever real at all

# Part III: The Return. The Orbit

It wasn't a fall.
It was a drift.
A slow, silent pull
back into her orbit
over the course of months.
No declarations.
No lightning.
Just gravity
doing what gravity does.
I circled from a distanc;
careful, measured,
keeping my warmth contained
so it wouldn't light anything she wasn't ready to see.
A message.
A visit.
A shared laugh over something small
that meant more to me than I'd admit.
Each time I got a little closer.
And each time,

I told myself
not to want more than what was offered.
But her world had a rhythm.
A pull.
And I couldn't stay away
without feeling like I'd left something behind.
So I came back.
Again and again.
Not to chase.
Not to fix.
Just to be where it felt right to be.
She never asked me to.
Never promised anything.
But she never pushed me away either.
And maybe that was enough.
Maybe I didn't need confirmation;
just the echo of what we once were,
wrapped in new light,
gentler than before.
We got closer.
Not all at once.
But like seasons shifting
in ways you only notice
when you stop and look back.
And suddenly, I was in her life again.
Not as a stranger.
Not as the man she used to know.

But as the one who stayed.
The one who never broke orbit.

# Part III: The Return. The Beauty That Hurt

It was slow.
Not a sudden laugh or a single moment;
but a series of soft returns.
A little more light in her voice.
More space between the heavy silences.
A joke dropped mid-conversation
that made her laugh before I could even respond.
And I felt it;
that fragile shift
from surviving
to living.
She was coming back.
Not to me.
Not for me.
But to herself.
And God, it was beautiful.
And God, it hurt.
Because I wanted to be the reason.
But I wasn't.

And maybe I never had been.
Still, I watched her glow
like someone who had once forgotten
what warmth felt like,
and was now learning how to hold it in her own hands
again.
And I smiled.
Meant it, even.
Because love,
real love,
doesn't need credit.
It just wants to see the other person whole.
So I stayed quiet.
Let her shine.
Let her heal
without reminding her of the ache she left in me.
And when I hung up the phone,
or walked away from another almost-moment,
I carried her happiness in my chest
like it was my own;
even as it echoed in the space
where she used to live.

# Part III: The Return. To Keep You Close

There were nights
when it almost slipped out.
Her voice on the other end of the line,
soft, familiar,
pulling pieces of me back into the light
without even trying.
We didn't see each other much back then.
Just phone calls.
Late ones.
The kind that stretch past midnight
because neither of you wants to hang up first.
And God,
that was all it took.
Just her voice.
Just the way she said my name
like it still belonged to someone safe.
I wanted to say it.
So many times.
I still love you.

I never stopped.
I've learned how to want you silently;
but it's never gotten easier.
But I didn't.
I let the words rise
then held them in the back of my throat
like a secret I was trying to starve.
Because I knew what it could ruin.
The fragile calm we'd built
from pain and patience and presence.
So I laughed when she laughed.
Listened when she vented.
Let her fill the air
with everything but the thing I longed to hear.
And every time the call ended,
I stared at the ceiling,
still holding the weight
of everything I hadn't said.
She never asked.
And maybe she already knew.
But that was the thing about love
the second time around;
it had to be quieter.
Gentler.
Held with care.
So I kept it in.
Not because it wasn't true;

but because sometimes,
not saying it
is the last way left to keep someone close.

# Part III: The Return. The Quiet We Chose

By then, we were close again.
Not like before;
but in a quieter, steadier way
that almost felt more dangerous.
She'd call, and I'd answer.
Not just the phone;
myself.
The version of me that only existed in her presence.
The man who never pretended
he didn't still care.
But I didn't say it.
Not out loud.
Because what we had
lived in the unsaid.
She'd laugh,
and I'd feel it in my chest.
Not the sound;
the way her joy still knew
exactly where to land inside me.

We'd talk late,
share things that felt like gifts
wrapped in casual tones.
But behind every word,
my heart leaned forward
just a little more.
And still;
I stayed quiet.
Because what if I ruined it?
What if naming it
shattered the careful balance we'd rebuilt?
So I swallowed it.
Every breath.
Every moment that begged for more
but settled for peace.
She never asked what I was feeling.
And I never made her.
Because love..real love..
sometimes lives
in what we choose not to say.
I wondered if she felt it too...
Or if I was the only one
drowning in the quiet
of everything
we never said.

# Part III: The Return. Even just This

I stopped needing more
a long time ago.
Stopped waiting for her to say it,
stopped watching for signs,
stopped expecting the story
to shift into something it never promised to be.
But I never stopped wanting to be near her.
Because some people
don't need to be yours
to still feel like home.
Her voice still softened the edges of my day.
Her laughter still landed
in the part of me
that always stayed open for her.
And some nights,
just hearing her say my name
was enough to keep me breathing
when everything else felt heavy.
I didn't reach.

Didn't ask.
Didn't ruin it
by dragging love into the room
when all she needed was friendship.
And still;
even in this quieter version of us,
even in the space between what we were
and what we'll never be;
her presence felt holy.
There's a kind of peace
in letting go of what you thought you needed
and realizing the person is still here,
just… differently.
It wasn't the dream.
But it was something.
And even just this;
her voice, her light, her nearness;
was more than I thought I'd ever get again.
So I held it.
Grateful.
Careful.
Quiet.
And tried not to want more
than what was already a gift.

# Part IV: The Breaking Point. Close Enough to Break

We were good at pretending.
Good at staying in the lines.
At sharing our days
and hiding our hearts
beneath laughter, tasks,
and the safety of "just friends."
We worked side by side;
hands dirty,
sun on our backs,
building things that felt
like more than just projects.
Plans spilled out between coffee and sawdust.
Dreams of land,
of space,
of maybe someday.
And I listened;
God, I listened;
to every word like it was a promise
we'd never say out loud.

I watched her sketch futures
in the air with her hands,
and even if I wasn't in them by name,
I was there.
Always there.
And it started getting heavy.
The longer I stayed close,
the harder it got
to hold back what was tearing through my chest.
Not because I wanted more from her;
but because everything in me
already belonged to her.
I wasn't starving for her body.
I was starving for clarity.
For a moment, a sign,
a look that said,
"Yes, I feel it too."
But I never asked.
Never leaned in.
Because her peace mattered more
than my need for answers.
So I kept showing up.
Drilling. Hauling.
Building whatever she needed.
Holding back the part of me
that just wanted to ask
if maybe, just maybe,

I was in the blueprints too.
We were close.
Closer than ever.
But I was starting to realize;
closeness isn't the same
as being chosen.
And I was close enough
to break.

# Part IV: The Breaking Point. The Turning

I was learning to vanish.
To become quiet
the way winter settles into the bones;
a life shrinking inward,
away from the world that never stayed.
That was the path I'd chosen:
isolation dressed as peace.
A horizon with no hands reaching.
And then;
you spoke of roots.
Not loudly,
just enough to make the air tremble.
A dream offered in pieces,
like a home imagined
before the foundation is laid.
A life that might be shared,
if only the winds changed.
I don't think you knew
what you were doing to me.

How those words made the ground shift beneath me,
how they scattered the frost in my chest
and made spring feel possible again.
I let go of exile.
I loosened my grip on the edges of the world.
Because for the first time,
your voice didn't sound like goodbye.
It sounded like maybe.
And maybe
was all it took
to undo the silence.
I spoke because I believed
you were already listening.
Because you cracked open the door,
and I;
I stepped through with every secret
I had taught myself to bury.
I wasn't chasing you.
I was answering a call
you may not have meant to make.
But once you speak of staying,
it's hard to keep pretending
you were never thinking of love.

# Part IV: The Breaking Point. The Pause Before The Truth

It didn't come in a wave.
Not a spark.
Not some movie-scene revelation.
Just a quiet ache
that had been growing for years
finally pressing hard enough
that I couldn't carry it alone anymore.
I remember sitting there;
phone in my hand,
but not calling.
Just staring at the quiet
that had started to feel too familiar.
I thought:
"If I don't say it soon,
it's going to rot inside me."
Because the longer I stayed silent,
the more it started to feel
like I was erasing parts of myself
just to keep the peace.

I didn't want to change anything.
Didn't want to win her.
I just needed her to know.
To really know.
What she meant.
What she had always meant.
Why every shared moment
felt stitched into something
I couldn't untangle.
I sat with it.
Held it like something sacred.
Not fragile;
but not careless either.
And in that pause,
between the thought and the truth,
I felt everything.
The risk.
The hope.
The possibility of losing her completely.
And still;
I picked up the pen.
Because some truths
aren't for fixing anything.

# Part IV: The Breaking Point. When I Wrote It Down

I couldn't say it out loud.
Not because I was afraid;
but because words felt too fragile
when I looked her in the eyes.
So I wrote it instead.
Not a confession.
Not a plea.
A truth.
That I loved her;
not blindly,
not instantly,
but because I had seen her.
Through years of friendship.
Through silence and laughter.
Through her strength,
and more importantly,
through the cracks she never tried to hide from me.
I told her I loved her
because of who she was;

not an idea,
not a version I imagined;
but the real, layered, imperfect, luminous her.
Her shadows didn't scare me.
Her fire didn't burn me.
I had stood beside all of it.
Witnessed it.
And I loved her because I had.
Not in some romantic haze.
But as a man who had come to know her
the way you know a season,
or the tide.
I could no longer carry it quietly.
I didn't ask her to change.
Didn't ask her to love me back.
I only asked her to know.
To really know
how deeply she was seen.
When I sealed the letter,
my hands were steady.
Because even if nothing changed,
I had told the truth.
And in the stillness that followed,
what hurt wasn't rejection.
It was the possibility
that something so carefully written
might have landed

on a heart not ready
to be understood.

# Part IV: The Breaking Point. What I Hoped She'd Say

I didn't expect fireworks.
Didn't expect her to show up at my door,
or call in tears saying she felt it too.
But I hoped;
quietly,
honestly,
that she'd read my words
and just... see me.
That she'd hear my heart
in the spaces between the sentences.
That she'd understand
I wasn't trying to change her world;
just offering the truth
of how deeply she shaped mine.
I hoped she'd pause.
Let it sink in.
Say something like,
"I didn't know... but now I do."
Or

"That must have taken a lot to write."
Or even just,
"I see you."
That would've been enough.
Not love returned.
Not a promise.
Just a moment of recognition.
A hand extended back
across the space I had finally crossed.
I hoped for gentleness.
For grace.
For a smile that said,
"You didn't ruin anything by telling me the truth."
But she didn't say those things.
Or anything like them.
And that's the part that hurts;
not that she didn't love me back,
but that she didn't seem to see
that I loved her without asking her to hold it.
That I only ever wanted her to know.

# Part IV: The Breaking Point. When the Silence Answered

It didn't come with a slam.
No harsh words.
No cruel reply.
Just… nothing.
And somehow,
that nothing
spoke louder than anything I'd hoped to hear.
She read it.
I know she did.
I felt the shift.
The quiet that followed wasn't absence;
it was decision.
The kind made in silence
when someone chooses not to respond,
because responding
means stepping closer.
And maybe she couldn't.
Or wouldn't.
Or just didn't feel the need to.

But God,
I kept checking.
My phone.
My thoughts.
That invisible thread
still stretched taunt between us.
Hoping for something;
not love.
Not even comfort.
Just... proof
that what I offered
had been received with care.
Instead, the quiet settled in.
Not like a blanket.
Like a bruise.
I didn't want a yes.
I didn't even want more.
I just wanted to know
that telling her the truth
hadn't broken the most sacred thing we had.
But the silence said it all.
And that's when I knew;
not that she didn't love me,
but that she didn't want to hold
what I had carried
for so long.

# Part IV: The Breaking Point. The Quiet Shift

I felt it
before she said a word.
Not a wall.
Not a goodbye.
Just something missing
where her warmth used to be.
Her laughter still showed up,
but late.
Her messages still came,
but shorter.
Her voice;
it didn't rise the way it used to
when she said my name.
She hadn't said anything outright.
But the rhythm was gone.
The ease.
The sense that I still lived
in the soft spaces of her life.
She was still there;

but she wasn't with me.
And I told myself
maybe I was imagining it.
Maybe it was just the aftershock
of being honest.
But deep down,
I knew something had changed.
That's when I wrote the second letter.
Not to fix anything.
Not to pull her back.
Just to give her the rest of it.
The part I hadn't said
the first time.
The part that said;
you've always mattered.
Even when you couldn't say it back.

# Part IV: The Breaking Point. What I Needed Her to Know

She hadn't read the second letter yet.
The one that carried everything;
the rest of the story,
the weight behind my silence,
the quiet love I had built
one moment at a time.
But I had already mailed it.
Sent it before we spoke.
Before I knew how much I'd need her
to see me clearly.
When we talked,
she only knew the first letter.
The soft version.
The beginning of the truth.
And something had shifted.
She didn't sound angry;
not exactly.
But there was distance in her voice,
a sharpness I hadn't heard from her before.

She was hurt, maybe.
Confused.
Protecting something I never meant to threaten.
She asked if it had all been real;
our friendship.
The years.
The closeness.
As if loving her meant
I had never valued what came before.
As if the depth of my heart
somehow erased the roots we grew from.
I wanted to explain.
To tell her;
it was never about replacing the friendship.
It was because of it.
But the conversation didn't leave space for that.
And I didn't want to push.
Didn't want to defend love
as if it were a crime.
So I listened.
Carefully.
Quietly.
And when we hung up,
all I could think about
was the second letter;
already moving toward her.
The letter that didn't ask for anything,

but offered everything.
Not to win her.
Not to fix what was changing.
Just to let her see
what had been true
for a very long time.
I don't know what happens next.
Not really.
But it feels like a dangerous place;
this silence between clarity and collapse.
And all I can do
is hope she opens it
with her whole heart.
Because what I needed her to know
was already on its way.

# Part V: The Days After.

## Seven Days

It's only been seven days.
That's what I keep telling myself.
Only seven.
But when your life
has been wrapped around someone else's presence;
their voice, their rhythm,
the sound of them just existing near you;
Seven days
is a lifetime with no air.
She hasn't written.
Hasn't called.
And I don't know
if the second letter ever even made it
into her hands.
I imagine her reading it.
Over and over.
Or not reading it at all.
I imagine her crying.
Or angry.

Or fine.
Maybe she's fine.
That one always hurts the most.
The days have blurred.
I eat,
I work,
I sleep; sort of.
But my mind
won't stop looping the sound of her voice
when she looked at my heart
and saw something dangerous instead of familiar.
I don't know where we stand now.
If there's even a we anymore.
She told me she didn't know
if we could be friends again.
And she said it like she meant it.
But seven days ago,
I still believed in us.
In what we built.
In the bond that had held
through more than most people ever understand.
Now it's quiet.
Not just in the room.
In my chest.
In the part of me that used to light up
just knowing she was in the world
and I wasn't alone in mine.

I don't know if she's thinking about me.
If she's angry.
If she's grieving.
All I know is;
I am.
Seven days.
And it already feels
Like after

# Part V: The Days After. The Days Don't End

Every morning feels like the same one.
The same weight behind my ribs.
The same thought:
Is today the day I stop hoping?
Seven days.
But the time doesn't pass like hours;
it folds in on itself.
Like a loop of breath I can't release.
I don't even know what I'm waiting for.
A message?
A sign?
Her voice?
Maybe just something
to prove I didn't lose her completely.
I stare at my phone
like it's holding its breath too.
I replay everything I said.
Every line in that second letter.
Was it too much?

Was it too soon?
Was it too true?
And even as I sit here aching,
I know I wouldn't take any of it back.
I had to say it.
Had to let her know
that my love wasn't built on want;
it was built on knowing her.
But I never expected
my truth to echo this long
without an answer.
And now the days blur.
They don't end.
They just... continue.
I wake up heavy,
work half-there,
eat without tasting,
sleep in fragments.
Everything is noise
except her silence.
People ask how I am.
I say, "Just tired."
Because how do you explain
that someone you've known for a decade
feels like a ghost you're still in love with?
I don't know where she is;
not just physically.

Emotionally.
Spiritually.
Is she thinking of me?
Is she angry?
Relieved?
Grieving?
Or is she gone?
I tell myself to be patient.
That she needs time.
That I need peace.
But nothing inside me
believes this
ends quietly.
And nothing inside me
knows
what happens next.

# Part V: The Days After. The Space Between

This is the part no one talks about;
the stretch of days
after the truth is spoken
but before the world tells you
what to do with it.
I haven't reached out.
And she hasn't either.
And so we sit,
invisible to each other,
but not gone.
There's a space between us now.
Not silence.
Not distance.
Something else.
Like a breath held too long.
Like a word never finished.
Like standing in a room
that used to feel like home,
but now the lights won't turn on.

I still see her everywhere.
In songs I skip.
In the way I pour my coffee.
In the conversations I almost start,
but don't.
People keep living.
They laugh.
They plan.
They ask if im ok
And I just nod,
because how do you say
you're stranded between a goodbye
and a maybe?
I don't know what she's feeling.
If the second letter made it.
If it softened anything,
or just dug the wound deeper.
I don't know if she's moved on,
or just...
paused.
I only know what I'm carrying.
Which is everything.
I'm not waiting.
Not exactly.
I'm just still here.
Still in it.
Still loving her

in the space between
what was
and whatever comes next.

# Part V: The Days After. What Remains

Strip everything away.
The calls,
the letters,
the years of unspoken meaning,
the shared futures half-built
and now left to rot in silence.
Take it all.
What's left?
Me.
Sitting here.
Alone with the echo of her name
rattling around my ribcage like it forgot
it's no longer welcome there.
There's no fight left.
No reach.
No logic I can twist into comfort.
Just the ache.
Just the truth.
I loved her.

With a quiet I didn't ask for.
With a loyalty that outlived its welcome.
With the kind of patience that scars.
And she walked away.
Not loudly.
But with enough silence
to make sure I heard it.
People say this kind of love is rare.
Sacred.
That it's better to have felt it
than not at all.
But right now,
it doesn't feel sacred.
It feels stupid.
Like a man standing in a burned-out church
clutching the ashes
and still calling it holy.
I didn't want to own her.
Didn't want to fix her.
I just wanted to be the one
who stayed when everyone else left.
But maybe that was never enough.
Maybe love,
even the kind built on friendship and fire,
still ends
like everything else.
And now?

Now it's quiet.
Not peaceful.
Not calm.
Just quiet.
And me inside it,
asking the only question that still matters:
If I gave her everything I had...
and she still let go...
what the hell do I do
with what's left of me?

# Part VI: The Seeing and the Staying. The Things She Didn't Know I Noticed

She never knew
how often I watched her without meaning to.
Not in awe;
in awareness.
Like someone memorizing the blueprint
of a place they already called home.
She didn't know
I noticed how she pressed her thumb
against her jaw when she was thinking;
like she was holding something in.
Or the way her shoulders dropped
when she finally let herself be comfortable.
How rare that was.
She didn't know
how her laugh changed when it was real.
How it cracked open the air
like something brighter was always hiding beneath her

waiting for permission to come out.
She never noticed
the way she spoke softer
when someone she loved walked into the room.
Or how fiercely she protected people
even when they didn't deserve it.
She didn't know
I watched her show up on hard days
without complaint,
without armor;
just a tired smile
and hands that kept moving.
She didn't see
the way she gave hope
without trying.
The way her presence
quieted something in me
I didn't know could be silenced.
She never knew
I could tell the difference
between her "I'm fine"
and her "I'm surviving."
And how many times
I chose not to say anything
because I knew she wouldn't want me to.
She didn't know
how often I looked at her

and thought,
"You don't have to be anything more than this."
And maybe that's what love really is;
not just seeing someone.
But noticing them
when they think no one is looking.
And choosing to stay.

# Part VI: The Seeing and the Staying. The Things I Hoped She Saw in Me

I never needed her to fix me.
But I always hoped
she saw how much I showed up.
Not in grand gestures;
just in the consistency.
In the way I stayed
even when I had every reason to leave.
I hoped she saw
how I carried her weight without asking her to lighten mine.
How I listened like it mattered;
because to me, it did.
Every word. Every pause. Every silence between.
I hoped she noticed
how calm I became around her.
How the noise in my head softened
when her voice was in the room.

That was never coincidence.
I hoped she saw
how I waited;
not impatiently,
but faithfully.
For the days she needed space.
For the moments she was distant.
For her to feel safe, not pushed.
I hoped she knew
how much I held back;
not because I was afraid,
but because I respected her pace
more than I needed my own relief.
I hoped she felt it
when I stood beside her in the quiet
and never asked her to be anyone
other than exactly who she was.
I never demanded to be chosen.
Never tried to trade friendship for something more.
But I hoped;
deep down;
that she saw
how the love I carried
was rooted in all the little things
she might've thought went unseen.
The tired moments she fought through.
The way she cared for people who didn't know how to

receive it.
The light she gave off
without even trying.
And maybe she did see it.
Maybe she just never said it.
Maybe it scared her.
Maybe it warmed her quietly from the inside.
I'll never know for sure.
But I lived that love honestly.
And I still hope
she saw it.
Even if she never said so.

# Part VI: The Seeing and the Staying. The Part of Me That Won't Let Go

There's a part of me
still curled up in the wreckage,
bleeding quietly
with no one left to witness.
But there's another part.
Smaller.
Angrier.
Harder to kill.
It doesn't care about fairness.
Doesn't need closure.
It just refuses
to let this be the end of me.
That part got me out of bed today.
It made coffee.
Put boots on.
Did the work, even with a hollow chest.
It didn't ask me to move on.

Didn't whisper hope or healing.
It just said:
"Stand the fuck up."
Not for her.
Not for love.
For me.
Because if I gave everything I had
and still lost her,
I sure as hell won't give her
the rest of me too.
That part doesn't want revenge.
It doesn't want to be numb.
It just wants to breathe again
without her name
pressing down on every inhale.
It wants to rebuild.
Not forget.
Never forget.
But to make something from this;
a life that isn't shaped
by someone else's silence.
And maybe it's just a whisper right now.
A flicker under all the grief.
But it's mine.
And it's still burning.

# Part VI: The Seeing and the Staying. What She Gave Me Without Knowing

She never promised anything.
Never said she'd stay.
Never claimed to be the kind of love
that finishes what it starts.
But still,
she gave me things I carry
every day.
She gave me the sound of laughter
that reminded me what light felt like
after too many heavy years.
She gave me stillness.
Not peace, exactly;
but that rare silence
where the world stopped asking me
to perform,
and I could just be.
She gave me presence.

The kind that doesn't fill the room with noise
but with weight.
That sense that someone saw you;
and chose to stand near.
She gave me belief.
Not in fate.
Not in fairy tales.
But in the idea
that maybe I wasn't too much
or too broken
or too late.
She gave me fire.
The kind that burns clean;
not out of anger,
but because it's real.
She gave me a mirror
I didn't recognize at first;
where I looked softer.
Less guarded.
More like the man
I had been trying to become
for years.
And she gave me the ache;
that sharp, holy ache
of loving something
I couldn't hold.
I'll never know

if she meant to.
If she saw what I became
in the gravity of her orbit.
If she knew what she stirred awake
just by sitting beside me.
But even now;
after all the silence,
after the letters,
after the distance hardened into truth;
I can still say this:
She changed me.
And she never even had to try.

# Part VI: The Seeing and the Staying. If You're Not Ready Yet

I saw the tremble in your gaze,
a truth you didn't try to hide—
not loud, not clear, but still it stays,
like morning tides that kiss the tide.

You didn't run, you didn't flee,
just stood where softer choices lie;
you met my heart, then let it be,
without the need to say goodbye.

You held it like a fragile thing,
not caged, not crushed, just understood
like birds you know aren't meant to cling,
but stay awhile if the branch is good.

You said you're not quite there, not now,
and I don't ask you to pretend.

I never needed some bold vow;
just that you wouldn't let it end.


You promised you would not explore
some echo that is not our song,
and though we're not what came before,
you've made me feel like I belong.

I said I think you feel this too;
you didn't flinch, you didn't fight.
You let the silence answer you
with something softer than the night.

And maybe that's the truest thing:
not "yes," not "no," but almost there;
like petals curled in early spring,
not rushed to bloom, but brave to care.

So if you're not yet ready, love,
then let me be the open gate;
I'll guard the stars you're dreaming of,
and I'll be patient with the wait.

Not waiting for you, like a cost;
but waiting with you, side by side.

For nothing we have built is lost;
and hope's a quiet place to hide.

# Reflection .

I didn't write these poems to win anyone back. I wrote them because I didn't know what else to do with the pieces of myself left over after loving someone in silence for so long.
This wasn't a fairytale.
There was no confession that turned into a kiss, no dramatic reunion on a rainy night.
There was just me.
And her.
And everything we never said.
But somewhere in all that ache,
I started finding parts of myself I didn't know I'd lost.
The man who keeps showing up.
The man who stays soft, even when it hurts.
The man who learns how to rebuild
without pretending the ruins never existed.
I still love her.
Not like I did in the beginning;
wild and wordless and full of hope.
But in the quiet way

you carry something sacred
even after you've set it down.
This book isn't a monument to heartbreak.
It's a record of endurance.
Of what it means to feel everything
and still stand back up.
Not to forget.
Not to move on.
But to live forward with all of it stitched into your chest
like proof that you were here.
And that you loved without needing to be loved back to
know it was real.

www.ingramcontent.com/pod-product-compliance
Lightning Source LLC
Chambersburg PA
CBHW060201050426
42446CB00013B/2937